TRANSWORLD PUBLISHERS 61–63 Uxbridge Road, London W5 5SA
A Random House Group Company www.transworldbooks.co.uk

First published in Great Britain in 2013 by Bantam Press
an imprint of Transworld Publishers

A CIP catalogue record for this book is available from the British Library.

ISBN 9780593071595

Addresses for Random House Group Ltd companies outside the UK can be found at:
www.randomhouse.co.uk The Random House Group Ltd Reg. No. 954009

Printed and bound in China

2 4 6 8 10 9 7 5 3 1

What it says on the cover.

Waldo Pancake

Completely blank page.

Coffee

I like having a coffee
and watching the
world go by.

That makes it sound
like I'm floating in
space while I'm having
my coffee.

I'm not, I'm in a coffee shop.

LOL

When someone's telling me a joke I'm too worried I won't find it funny to be able to listen properly, so even if it is I'm still faking a laugh at the end.

Forward slashes look like rain.

People

If I'm in a group of people
and we're all having a
chat, and then suddenly
everyone walks off
and leaves me with only
one person who I don't
know, I also just walk off.

You know thought bubbles? What if you were thinking about bubbles.

People only say they'll
be five minutes because
they've got that many
fingers.

If we all had three
there'd be less
waiting around.

Flying

When I'm queuing to get off
a plane, I watch how the
stewardess says goodbye
to the people in front of me,
and she's never as smiley to
me as she is to them.

Nostrils

You know when it hits you how weird something you take for granted is? I did that with nostrils today. After that, everyone I looked at made me feel sick walking around with their disgusting plug-socket noses.

Men called Guy
are just walking
around confusing
people.

You don't get
women called Girl.

How random
is people's use
of the word
random.

Undo

I've started thinking I can undo
mistakes in real life like I can on
my computer. Also, if I've lost
something, for a second I think
I can do a Google search.

I accidentally ate the
sticker on my apple.
My poo came out
with the sticker on it.

What's with the
no leg room at the
cinema?

I wish my legs were
detachable. I'd
unscrew them and
put them in the
drinks holders.

Envy

I walked past a restaurant today and got jealous of the people eating, so I went in and suddenly the people walking past looked like they were having more fun.

They should get rid of windows in restaurants.

Sometimes I wonder how many more phones I'll have before I die.

Why don't we just call all days Saturday, and have the number after it?
e.g. 'Today is Saturday number 27.'

How much hassle is hair.

You know on YouTube when people write 'OMG 0:48!' because they liked what happened at 0:48 in the video?

I do that, but in reference to my lifespan.

e.g. 'OMG 10:6:4:13:22:06!' refers to when I was ten and I had Chicken Kiev and chips for tea (my fave).

The phrase 'who knew?' has really taken off.

Who knew?

Celery

I was in the supermarket today and saw some celery and this got me thinking about celery. Like when a worker in a celery factory goes to the boss to talk about his salary the boss probably thinks he's saying celery. The worker probably says no I said salary but the boss still hears celery, such is his involvement with the vegetable. It probably goes on for hours like this.

eye
eye
nose
mouth
ear
ear

Why are my ears, nostrils, mouth and eyes dotted around all over my head?

They should be lined up along one side like the USB ports on my computer.

What's with the always
having to go up and down
stairs?

You'd think they'd have
flattened everything out
by now*

*idea for standup routine.

That. Is. SO.
Funny.

why aren't
you laughing
then

Being green

When I'm in a coffee shop I always take a massive handful of napkins then when I get home I recycle them without so much as a lip wipe. You've got to do your bit, haven't you.

If I'm walking down the street and I see a drain, I get the urge to slot my phone down it. Same if I see a pint of beer, I want to dunk it in.
If I hear armageddon is coming, I might treat myself and do it.

Downside: wouldn't be able to make farewell calls.

Tear page to cover noise of cough.

Not funny

I'm not being funny, but when someone says 'I'm not being funny,' what they say after it is never funny.

Why do we only use pizza cutters for cutting pizzas, then for everything else go back to boring old non-rotating knives?

That killed a page.

Friends

I hate it when you recognize someone from a distance and have to walk towards them keeping your face looking all pleased and excited.

Yes, I do know what you mean. Stop asking me.

Who
writes
this
crap

Feel a bit bad now.
It's not really crap.

Also available in ebook*

Be happy

People used to say to me,
'Cheer up it might never happen!'
but they've stopped now.
Maybe it happened?

Sarcasm

Ooh, sarcasm is the lowest form of wit. Yeah, at least I'm on the wit scale?

Why do people always
ask if you want a nice
cup of tea?
Ooh, I couldn't have
a horrible one could I?

How it's going

Have you seen it when someone says 'How's it going?' to someone and the person says 'How's it going' back? It's like nobody actually wants to know how it's going.

I saw one of those posters that say

Why not have a coffee & a muffin

so I went up and told them.

I could've
tweeted
all of this.

Ashoo

When someone sneezes it sounds like they're saying 'A shoe!' all excitedly, so I always go, 'Where?' and look around, also excitedly.

Morning

When I see someone in the morning I say 'Morning.'
Same if I see them in the evening, except I say 'Evening.'
I'm just stating what time of day it is.

I feel sorry for W. He had it easy, hanging out
up there with X & Z, then along came the internet.

Explanashe: W isn't used all that much as a letter, as aren't X & Z, but now it's used all the time what with www.thisandthat.com

Thanks

People don't appreciate how much I've shortened my thankyous.

They think I'm saying 'kyou', but I've got it down to 'q'.

Pimp your Meh

Event in a coffee shop

Taking the lid off my cappuccino, I saw that all the chocolate powder had stuck to the inside of it along with half the froth. 'WHAT'S THE POINT?' I screamed, dropping to my knees in exasperation. Luckily they both landed on full sugar sachets that'd been dropped earlier.

Scene from bonkbuster I'm working on.

Phones'll be as thin as this page soon.

Amazing innit.

Prob a bit too thin though innit.

Turn pages much?

I've had it up to here
with junk mail.
You can't tell how high
I've had it up to from
that, of course.
It's about halfway up
my forehead.

News

Saw someone receiving
terrible news on the
phone in the street
the other day.
Was quite jealous
that they were getting
it out of the way.

You have enough stuff*

*apart from this book.

Honesty

People who say 'to be honest'
make me think everything else
they're saying is a lie, to be
honest.

Poo

If the phrase 'touch wood' was 'touch poo', I reckon there'd be loads less superstitious people.

Thinks

I was walking downstairs with a friend the other day when we saw a 'Mind your head' sign. 'And subsequently your mind!' I said, and my friend chuckled, then I hit my head.

I hate goodbyes.
Not so keen on
hellos either.
That bit in the
middle's a
hassle too.

Thanks for reading
this book, not that
anyone has.